THE
HOURS
THAT
REMAIN

THE HOURS THAT REMAIN

KEITH BARKER

PLAYWRIGHTS CANADA PRESS

TORONTO

PLAYWRIGHTS CANADA PRESS
202-269 Richmond St. W., Toronto, ON M5V 1X1
416.703.0013 • info@playwrightscanada.com • www.playwrightscanada.com

We acknowledge the financial support of the Canada Council for the Arts, the Ontario Arts Council (OAC), the Ontario Media Development Corporation, and the Government of Canada through the Canada Book Fund for our publishing activities.

 Canada Council
for the Arts
Conseil des arts
du Canada

ONTARIO ARTS COUNCIL
CONSEIL DES ARTS DE L'ONTARIO

an Ontario government agency
un organisme du gouvernement de l'Ontario

Canada Ontario
Ontario Media Development
Corporation

Cover painting, *Untitled*, by Travis Murphy
Book design by Blake Sproule

LIBRARY AND ARCHIVES CANADA CATALOGUING IN PUBLICATION
Barker, Keith (Keith N.)
     The hours that remain / Keith Barker.

Issued also in electronic format.
ISBN 978-1-77091-135-2

     I. Title.

PS8603.A73557H68 2013   C812'.6   C2012-907945-6

First edition: May 2013. Second printing: January 2017.
Printed and bound in Canada by Marquis Book Printing, Montreal

To all of the women who raised me.

The Hours That Remain was first produced by New Harlem Productions and Saskatchewan Native Theatre Company at Studio 914 in Saskatoon from October 4 to October 14, 2012, and as the inaugural production at the new Aki Studio in the Daniels Spectrum Building in Toronto from October 19 to November 3. The production featured the following cast and creative team:

Denise: Tara Beagan
Dan: Eli Ham
Michelle: Keira Loughran

Directed by David Storch
Stage management by Richard Cliff
Costume and prop design by Isidra Cruz
Set and projection design by Andy Moro
Choreography by Monique Diabo
Lighting design by Michelle Ramsay
Sound design by Samuel Sholdice

Please note that all of the female parts are played by the Michelle Winters character except for Denise Winters, who plays herself.

CHARACTERS

Denise Winters
Michelle Winters
Daniel Koop
Laney Menard
Loraine Major
Sandra Williams

We begin in the dark. It's the wind we hear first, with the sounds of the forest at night. Now there are crickets, and then a transport truck approaching from the horizon. It's as if we are standing along the Trans-Canada Highway with our eyes shut. The truck passes us and slowly fades away. The stars come out, and then the sound of warm whispers permeates the air. They blend into a cacophony of sound. At its crescendo everything shatters into silence followed by the systematic snuffing out of the stars and we are back in black again. Lights snap back on. We are in DANIEL *and* DENISE's *house.* DANIEL *is sitting watching television.* DENISE *enters. She stands looking out the window for a long time.*

DANIEL   She'll be here.

Silence.

Well, waiting at the window isn't going to make it happen any quicker.

DENISE I know.

DANIEL I'm just saying—

DENISE Daniel, she was supposed to be here by six. It's almost six thirty.

DANIEL You sound surprised. Your sister is never on time.

DENISE I told the girls we'd be there for seven.

DANIEL So what? You know for a fact none of them will show up before seven thirty.

He looks up and sees her as if for the first time.

Oh wow… You look good.

DENISE You're just saying that.

DANIEL No I'm not.

She smiles and goes over to him. They kiss. She pulls away.

DENISE What do you think of this shirt?

DANIEL It looks good to me.

DENISE You're right. I'm going to change it.

She leaves to change.

DANIEL   What?

DENISE   Which do you think looks better, my red shirt or my blue sweater?

DANIEL   I like what you're wearing now—

DENISE   —Daniel.

DANIEL   I don't know. The red shirt?

MICHELLE enters in a hurry. She is wearing her work clothes from the diner.

MICHELLE Hey.

DANIEL   Hey.

MICHELLE Where is she?

DANIEL   Upstairs getting ready.

MICHELLE *(to DENISE)* Sorry I'm late!

DENISE   *(from off)* Mich? What happened?

MICHELLE It's Marty. She was late for work again! I don't know what's wrong, but this is the fourth time this month. Anyways, I had to cover her tables until she showed up.

DENISE   Is she okay?

MICHELLE Yeah I think so.

DENISE   I'll be down in a second, I'm just changing my shirt.

MICHELLE   Take your time.

DANIEL   So, girls' night, eh?

MICHELLE   Don't even joke about it.

DANIEL   I'm surprised.

MICHELLE   Yeah, so am I. Dee caught me in a moment of weakness.

DANIEL   You know there's a Habs game on tonight? Dale and Vic
            are coming over.

MICHELLE   Seriously?

DANIEL   Yeah, puck drops at seven thirty.

MICHELLE   I totally forgot! You think she'd let me stay and watch
            the game?

DANIEL   Good luck with that. She's been talking about this all
            week.

MICHELLE   Daniel, I have nothing in common with these women.
            All they talk about is their kids, their husbands, and the
            fact that none of them are having any sex. I hate girls'
            night.

DANIEL   I know, but it means a lot to her.

MICHELLE   Maybe I can fake sick.

DANIEL   Hey, leave me out of it.

DENISE enters wearing the blue sweater.

DENISE   Ready to go?

DANIEL   Hey, what happened to the red shirt?

DENISE   The blue looks better with jeans.

DANIEL   Whatever.

MICHELLE   I don't know about tonight, Dee, I'm feeling a bit under the weather.

DENISE   Oh no, are you okay?

MICHELLE   I feel like I'm starting to come down with something, you know? Like I've got a tickle in the back of my throat.

DENISE   That doesn't sound so good. Maybe you caught a bit of the hockey-itis?

MICHELLE   The what?

DENISE   Or is it the Habs flu? You'll probably feel better after the puck drops at seven thirty.

MICHELLE   Dee—

DENISE   I heard everything from upstairs.

MICHELLE   I'm better with guys, you know that—

DENISE   You promised me you would come out tonight.

MICHELLE   I know, but it's a Habs game.

DENISE   So what? There's always a Habs game on. This is one
                night out with the girls.

MICHELLE   But the Habs are playing the…

She hits DANIEL *for help.*

DANIEL   Bruins—

MICHELLE   Bruins! It's an important game.

DENISE   Don't do this to me. I've been looking forward to this
                all week. It's supposed to be fun.

MICHELLE   It will be… for you.

DENISE   You promised.

DENISE *gives her sister that look that makes it very hard to say no.*

MICHELLE   …Fine, I'll go. But if anyone asks me why I'm not mar-
                ried yet, or if I'm considering having any kids, then I'm
                out of there.

DENISE   That's not fair.

MICHELLE   You're right, it's not. Just because I'm not married
                doesn't mean I'm looking for a husband. And not every
                woman needs to have a baby to be fulfilled.

DANIEL   Dee, It's almost seven.

DENISE   Right, we'd best be off then.

MICHELLE   Right, we don't want to keep the girls waiting!

DENISE   Hey, if you're going to be like that then don't come.

MICHELLE   Oh come on, I'm joking.

DENISE   Yeah, funny stuff. *(to DANIEL)* Anyways, I'll call you later.
           We'll probably catch a cab home.

DANIEL and DENISE kiss.

DANIEL   *(mockingly to MICHELLE)* Have fun.

MICHELLE   You're loving this, aren't you?

DENISE   Let's go.

*The two ladies exit. DANIEL sits back down at the television.
MICHELLE pops her head back in.*

MICHELLE   Pst. I'll be back for the third period.

Lights out. Shift. Lights up on MICHELLE outside of her car.

Stupid piece of American-made junk! I know, I know, I
should have and I was going to bring you into the shop
when I heard that knocking sound. But I just had you
in there last week! I mean, if it's not the alternator then
it's the oil pressure, and if it's not the battery then it's
the transmission. Now what? I can't imagine since I just
put a THOUSAND DOLLARS into you! That's a lot of mon-
ey on a waitress' salary! Not to mention the tow truck
you're about to cost me... I don't get it... What did I
do wrong? I respected you— I treated you well. An oil
change every what? five thousand kilometres: check.
Wheel alignment and rotation: check. Change the air
filter once a year: check. The odd car wash: check. Tire

pressure: check. I even changed your windshield-wiper blades. But oh no, it's not enough. No, you decide to break down on the side of the highway after a very long day of work.

We hear a transport truck approaching. MICHELLE *starts waving.*

Oh! Please stop. Please, please stop! I'll love you forever! I will I will I will! Yes? Yes! Sorry, babe, but I'm going to have to take this one. Don't worry, I'll a send a tow truck for you right away… Yeah, I love you too.

MICHELLE *exits. We hear the truck pull away. Shift. We are back at* DANIEL *and* DENISE'S *house. A woman can be heard half humming/half singing the song "You Are My Sunshine."* DANIEL *is drawn onto the stage by the sounds of her singing. He remembers a better time.* DENISE *enters wearing a bathrobe. A towel is wrapped up in her hair.* DANIEL *is stunned.*

DENISE   Morning. Did you have breakfast yet?

Beat.

DANIEL   No.

DENISE   What's up?

Beat.

DANIEL   Nothing.

DENISE   Then why are you looking at me like that?

DANIEL   Like what?

DENISE   Like someone died.

DANIEL   Sorry.

DENISE   Don't be. You look lost.

DANIEL   Really?

DENISE   Yes really.

            (*She goes over to him.*) You okay?

DANIEL   Yeah…

DENISE   I hope my singing didn't bother you.

DANIEL   No. I love it when you sing.

DENISE   Good, 'cause it was for you.

            (*She kisses him.*) Don't worry, I'll clean up the water.

DANIEL   Sorry?

DENISE   I know you don't like it when I leave water on the floor.
            I just wanted to see you.

DANIEL   I don't care about the water.

DENISE   Hey, what's wrong?

DANIEL   Nothing.

DENISE   Are you sure?

DANIEL   Yeah.

He grabs her and hugs her desperately.

          I missed you.

DENISE   *(She smiles.)* Uh huh.

DANIEL   I really missed you.

DENISE   *(She laughs.)* You are so funny sometimes.

She kisses him and walks out. He is left stunned.

          Hey, cowboy, Are you coming or what?

DANIEL   I'll be right there!

          (He looks up.) Thank you.

DANIEL runs after her. Shift. MICHELLE and DENISE enter. DENISE is carrying a grocery bag with dog food in it.

MICHELLE   Why are you telling me this?

DENISE   Because you're my sister.

MICHELLE   Exactly. I'm not your marriage counsellor.

DENISE looks hurt.

          (sighs) Go on…

DENISE   *(As she speaks she puts away the dog food.)* So yes-
          terday, I asked Daniel to pick up dog food on his way

home from work. He said, "Sure, not a problem." So, this morning I go to feed the dog and, lo and behold, there's no dog food. I ask him, "Daniel where's the dog food?" He says, "There's no dog food? Dee, you should have told me, I would have picked some up yesterday on my way home from work."

MICHELLE   Men are all the same, Dee.

DENISE   Seriously, I want to strangle him sometimes, you know? It's like—take notes if you can't keep up—

MICHELLE   You married him—

DENISE   —And pick up your dirty clothes. I'm not your mother—

MICHELLE   Hey, did wonder boy tell you about the fight we had on Thursday?

DENISE   No.

MICHELLE   He didn't mention it?

DENISE   No, why?

MICHELLE   Ah, man, your husband is something special.

DENISE   What do you mean?

MICHELLE   Like the Olympics.

DENISE   Hey now.

MICHELLE   Relax, I'm joking. But Daniel, wow, is he ever pissed at me right now.

DENISE   Oh, Michelle, what did you do to him?

MICHELLE What did I do?

DENISE   Don't act all innocent. I know you like to push his buttons.

MICHELLE Oh, come on. He does the exact same thing to me.

DENISE   Just tell me what happened.

MICHELLE Fine. So we stop in at Stan's after helping Flossie stack her wood for the winter, and, get this, he orders a SCONE and ham sandwich.

DENISE   He did not!

MICHELLE He did too!

DENISE   He's never done that with me before.

MICHELLE Well he did it with me.

DENISE   You're kidding, right? He didn't call them SCONES.

MICHELLE YES, he did. And I'll have you know I politely corrected him. I said, "Daniel it's a SCON not a SCONE."

Out steps DANIEL.

DANIEL   Not where I'm from it's not. It's a SCONE.

MICHELLE Well everyone else calls them by their proper name, which is SCON. It's pretty basic English there, buddy.

DANIEL   Basic English.

MICHELLE   Yeah, you wouldn't call a cookie a cock-ee, would you?

DANIEL   That doesn't make any sense.

MICHELLE   You know who calls them SCONES? Losers call them *SCONES*!

DANIEL   Do I look like a loser to you?

MICHELLE   Do I have to answer that question?

DANIEL   And you wonder why you're single.

MICHELLE   No, I wonder why my sister settled.

DANIEL   Says the person who's been single all of her life.

MICHELLE   Yeah, I guess I'm just lucky that way.

(*to DENISE*) Now at this point, everyone in the restaurant has heard our conversation and they giggle every time he calls them SCONES, and the more he calls them SCONES the more people giggle, and the more people giggle the more upset he gets, until finally—

DANIEL   (*He jumps up and addresses everyone.*) How do you spell the word CONE?

MICHELLE   Why?

DANIEL   C-O-N-E. If you add an s to CONE, what do you get—I'll tell you what you get, you get SCONE! It's pretty basic English there, buddy! Cone with an s!

MICHELLE   You're being juvenile…

DANIEL   No, apparently I'm being a loser! Or is it *low*-ser to everyone else in the world?

MICHELLE *(to DENISE)* Then he grabbed his coat and stormed out.

He storms out.

DENISE   He did not!

MICHELLE He did too! Not to mention that he left me at the restaurant, so I had to ask Anita for a ride home.

DENISE   You have to be nicer him.

MICHELLE No, he has to learn how to take a joke— Wait a sec, what time is it?

DENISE   I don't know.

          (She looks at a clock on the wall.) …Just after three o'clock.

MICHELLE Damn, I've got to go. I said I'd pick Marty up from work.

DENISE   Oh, that's nice of you. How is she doing?

MICHELLE Willy ran off with their neighbour, how do you think she's doing?

DENISE   I can't believe that, and they have two kids.

MICHELLE I know, terrible. Anyways, call me tomorrow and we'll figure something out for the weekend.

They hug. MICHELLE leaves. DANIEL walks in from the kitchen.

DENISE   *(to MICHELLE)* No, you call me. You never answer your
           phone.

DANIEL   Hey, who you talking to?

DENISE   What?

DANIEL   Oh, weird. I could have sworn I heard other voices.

DENISE   You did.

DANIEL   I did?

DENISE   Yeah, it was Michelle.

DANIEL   *(laughs)* Very funny.

DENISE   I'm serious. And just so you know, she told me about
           the fight.

DANIEL   The fight.

DENISE   Yeah, the one you had at Stan's.

DANIEL   What are you talking about?

DENISE   Stop playing stupid. You two had a fight—

DANIEL   At Stan's—

DENISE   Yeah, she called you a loser.

DANIEL   Yeah, well, she used to call me a lot of things. She was
           good at that… You're not talking about the time when
           I left her at the restaurant?

DENISE   Yes.

DANIEL   That was five years ago.

DENISE   Daniel, I'm serious.

DANIEL   So am I.

DENISE   You stacked wood for Flossie.

DANIEL   Yeah, then we went to Stan's—

DENISE   Yes, you went to Stan's—

DANIEL   What were we fighting about?

DENISE   Don't even get me started—

DANIEL   SCONES! That's what it was… Yeah, I won that one. Then
            she started throwing food at me.

DENISE   Scones. You're sure?

DANIEL   Yeah. It was the last time I saw her alive— Sorry.

DENISE   But she was just here.

DANIEL   Dee—

DENISE   —She was.

DANIEL   I think you might be mixing things up again.

        Silence.

Hey, *I'm* here.

DENISE   Uh huh.

DANIEL   Oh, that isn't good enough?

DENISE   Of course it is.

DANIEL   I'll take that, even half-heartedly.

DENISE   Daniel, please.

DANIEL   Don't worry, it's just my feelings. It's not like I'm used to it or anything.

DENISE   I'm sorry, but she was…

She is lost in the moment.

Beat.

DANIEL   What?

Beat.

DENISE   …Sorry?

DANIEL   She was what?

DENISE   (*She finds herself again.*) She *was* here… Michelle. Just now.

DANIEL   Listen, I didn't want to say this before, but I was on this website the other day that said it's quite common for people to experience hallucinations and separation trauma when dealing with a missing loved one.

DENISE   But she was real, Daniel. She hugged me when she left.

DANIEL   I don't know what to say.

DENISE   Why don't you believe me?

DANIEL   Because… We need to be logical about this. She disappeared over five years ago, right? We haven't heard a word from her. Why would she show up in our living room all of a sudden?

DENISE   I don't know.

DANIEL   See? It doesn't make any sense. Maybe you were daydreaming.

DENISE   That's not funny.

DANIEL   I'm not joking. It's pretty traumatic stuff, right? You see her in everything you do. You're constantly going through all of your memories, looking for any clues about her disappearance.

DENISE   I'm telling you she was real, Daniel, as real as you are to me now.

DANIEL   I know. I miss her too.

Beat.

DENISE   Daniel?

DANIEL   What?

DENISE   Do you think she'll come back?

DANIEL   Stop, please stop—

DENISE   —But she was here—

DANIEL   —No, stop. We've been through this a hundred times.
          It doesn't get us anywhere.

Beat.

DENISE   Yeah.

DANIEL   Hey, look at me. *(He smiles.)* Why don't you come have
          some dinner?

DENISE   Okay… I just need a moment.

DANIEL   Sure…

DANIEL makes his way back to the kitchen.

          But don't wait too long, okay? You don't want to be
          eating this cold. I made your favourite tonight: venison
          with all the trimmings.

DENISE   Since when do you cook dinner?

DANIEL   Whoa, whoa! That's not fair; I cook!

DENISE   No, you barbecue, that's different…

As this is happening a woman walks out. She is a sex-trade worker. She notices DENISE *but* DENISE *is not aware of her presence. The woman asks her a question. We cannot hear the question. She continues to speak. We cannot hear her until her lines below.*

DANIEL   Different how?

DENISE   Throwing meat on a grill and calling it supper is not cooking.

DANIEL   Says you! Man has done it since the dawn of time. Besides, you love it when I barbecue. And for your information, this venison was cooked in the oven... with potatoes.

MICHELLE   Excuse me—

DENISE   Mich!

MICHELLE   Sorry?

DENISE   Daniel, come here for a second.

To MICHELLE.

He doesn't think you're real—Daniel!

MICHELLE   Who are you talking to?

DENISE   Seriously, if you think I'm making this up then get out here and see for yourself!

DENISE *touches the woman, checking to see if she is in fact real.*

MICHELLE   (*MICHELLE bats her hand away.*) Whoa! What are you
           strung out on?

DENISE   Daniel!

MICHELLE   Hey! I just need a light! Then you can get back to doing
           whatever it is you're doing, all right?

DENISE   Since when do you smoke?

MICHELLE   Excuse me? Do I know you?

DENISE   (*laughs*) Do you know me?

MICHELLE   Yeah, do I know you?

DENISE   Mich, it's me.

MICHELLE   Me who?

DENISE   Seriously, Mich.

MICHELLE   Listen, you call me Mich one more time and I'll mess
           up that pretty little face of yours, okay?

DENISE   Uh, okay.

MICHELLE   You obviously have the wrong person. Name's Trixie.

DENISE   (*trying to contain a laugh*) Trixie?

MICHELLE   Yeah, Trixie. You got a problem with that?

DENISE   No, of course not. Trixie is a good name.

MICHELLE Yeah, thanks. Now do you have a light Ms....

The woman gestures for a name to end the sentence with.

DENISE Dee—Denise. And no, sorry, I don't... Trixie.

MICHELLE Stop saying my name.

DENISE Sorry.

MICHELLE And don't say sorry—

DENISE Sorry, Trixie.

The woman just glares at DENISE *until she looks away. Silence.*

MICHELLE So, has it been busy?

DENISE Busy?

MICHELLE Yeah. Has there been much traffic?

DENISE Oh, sorry, I haven't been paying much attention.

MICHELLE Really?

DENISE Really.

MICHELLE How long have you been out here?

DENISE Oh, I just got here.

MICHELLE No, how long have you been OUT HERE?

DENISE I'm sorry?

MICHELLE   Turning tricks.

DENISE   Tricks? Oh— OHHH.

MICHELLE   This isn't your first night, is it?

DENISE   No.

MICHELLE   *(sighs)* Come over here.

DENISE hesitates.

Come here!

DENISE immediately walks over to her. The woman starts fixing her up.

You look more like a mother. You may want to spruce things up, if you know what I mean.

DENISE   Yeah.

MICHELLE   Let me give you some free advice, okay? Look at me, I'm serious. I don't care what your vice is, just don't do it with the customers. When you first get in the car grab his crotch. If he pushes your hand away he's a cop: get out. Get payment first. Start high then negotiate from there, but start high. Go with your instincts: if it doesn't feel right, take a pass. Don't get into a car with more than one person. Make sure you're as comfortable as you can be in the situation, and never give up control. Be firm, they like that. Always know the best way to escape. And do not under any circumstances drink or take anything that is given to you.

DENISE starts to get upset.

> Listen, this isn't for everyone. It's nothing to be ashamed of. Maybe you shouldn't be out here.

DENISE   Maybe *you* shouldn't be out here.

MICHELLE   Do you have anyone you can call?

We hear the sounds of a truck pulling up as the headlights flash by them. MICHELLE poses for the truck as it passes by. The truck stops and MICHELLE gets the nod from the driver. She starts to walk over but stops herself.

> You want this one?

DENISE   No.

MICHELLE goes to leave.

> Please don't go.

MICHELLE   Sorry, sister, but I've got a kid to support.

DENISE   Please?

MICHELLE stops. She pulls out a pen and a piece of paper and starts writing.

MICHELLE   Listen, this is the address to my apartment. My mom will be there. Tell her I sent you. She's great. You can stay the night if you want, and then can get yourself sorted out in the morning, okay? I'll be home later. Go.

She hands it to DENISE.

DENISE   But there's no address here, it's just a number.

The truck honks.

MICHELLE Hey! What does this look like, a drive-through?! Hold your horses!

Back to her.

          I'll swing by later, okay?

The woman leaves. We hear the truck pull away as the lights fade.

DENISE   But how do I know what street you live on?

She looks at the paper and then pockets it as DANIEL enters holding cutlery and walks to the other side of the stage. He doesn't stop to talk and walks off stage.

DANIEL   Sorry?

DENISE   Daniel? What are you doing here?

DANIEL   It's my house, I live here... And someone has to set the dinner table.

DENISE   Dinner?

DANIEL walks back in.

DANIEL   Yeah, dinner, remember? You, me, some slightly overcooked venison and somewhat burnt potatoes—

DENISE   Stop it—

DANIEL   A bottle of wine, maybe some nudity later on?

DENISE   She came back.

DANIEL   Who?

DENISE   Michelle.

DANIEL   When? I've been here the whole time.

DENISE   I'm telling you she was here. I called for you.

He gives her a look of exasperation.

Why don't you believe me?

DANIEL   I'm trying, I really am.

DENISE   Are you?

DANIEL   Yes.

DENISE   'Cause it doesn't feel like it.

DANIEL   Look at it from my end… I go into the kitchen, and
            when I come out, Michelle has apparently visited you.
            Right, so I go back into the kitchen, and when I return,
            Michelle has again paid a visit to you. You say you called
            me but I didn't hear anything. Both happen in the span
            of a few minutes. Does she only make an appearance
            when I'm out of the room? I mean, come on. Oh here,
            let's try this.

DANIEL runs out of the room and back in again.

Anything?

DENISE   That's not funny, Daniel.

DANIEL   I'm not trying to be funny. Okay, maybe a little bit, but seriously, did she appear again?

She gives him a look. He tries again, running out and back in again.

What about now?

He runs out and back in again.

What about now?

DENISE   Please stop it. I'm not stupid.

DANIEL exits one last time.

What about—

This time a woman enters. She is in business attire. Her lipstick has been smudged. She is dishevelled.

MICHELLE   —Excuse me!

DENISE   *(DENISE is surprised.)* Michelle! Daniel, it worked! Are you all right?

MICHELLE   I'm sorry, but I've been mugged. Please help me.

DENISE goes to her sister and tries to help her.

DENISE   What happened? Daniel!

MICHELLE   I was putting some stuff in the back seat of my car when two guys jumped me.

DENISE   Give me a second, I'm listening. Daniel?!

MICHELLE   You don't know where there's a pay phone, do you?

DENISE   No, I'm sorry, but you can use our phone if you want…

DENISE can't find it.

MICHELLE   I used to roll my eyes at people when they told me to buy pepper spray for when I'm working late. All I could think about when it was happening was, "Dammit! I should have had something with me." I thought they were going to rape me, I really did—Look, I'm shaking.

She shows her hands.

DENISE   How did you get away?

MICHELLE   Um… I, uh, I, uh, I walked up to my car like I always do and opened the back door to put my briefcase in. And out of nowhere this guy grabs me from behind and pushes me headfirst into the back seat and pins me down. I had a box full of stuff in the back seat, stuff meant for the Sally Ann. So I manage to reach into the box and grab my old iron. I swing it behind me as hard as I can, and I hit the guy right in the side of the head with it. Blood everywhere! He jumps out of the car holding his face, screaming his head off, and this other guy—must have been his partner or something—is just standing there stunned. So I start swinging it at him, and he runs around to the other side of the car.

So I chase him with it like a crazy person. Then I get caught up in the cord and he slips into the driver's seat. I don't know how he got my keys but he ends up starting my car. At that point I'm hysterical, and he's really scared, and he keeps trying to get the car into gear. I must have hit the window five times before he took off in reverse— Almost ran over his friend. And before I could do anything, the other one jumps in and they're gone. Left me standing there with nothing but this old iron and blood all over my clothes.

DENISE   Well, at least you're all right.

MICHELLE   (*She cheers with the iron.*) Yeah, here's to my health.

We hear the sound of a transport truck pull up and wait.

Is that for you?

DENISE   Uh… No.

MICHELLE doesn't move.

Are you all right?

MICHELLE   No. I feel like I've been shaken so hard I can't find my balance.

DENISE   Well, I'm here now.

MICHELLE   I don't understand. What is that truck waiting for?

DENISE   I don't know. It's probably nothing.

MICHELLE   What if it's them?

DENISE   You don't have to worry, there are two of us now.

MICHELLE   No, it's three.

DENISE   No, I mean there are two of us now.

MICHELLE   *(in a panic)* Three. I said I was three. I've got to go, I'm
                   sorry, I've got to keep moving.

She starts to leave.

DENISE   I think it's better if we stick together.

MICHELLE   I... I... I can't stay here. You shouldn't either!

MICHELLE runs off in a panic.

DENISE   Michelle! Michelle!

The truck pulls away quickly and fades. DANIEL reappears.

DANIEL   Denise?

DENISE   Where did she go?

DANIEL   Who?

DENISE   My sister.

DANIEL   What are you talking about?

DENISE   Michelle, she was just here.

DANIEL   Where have you been?

DENISE   What do you mean?

DANIEL   Are you kidding me?!

DENISE   Listen to me—

DANIEL   NO, you listen to me. It's been over TWO WEEKS since
          I heard from you.

DENISE   Daniel, please—

DANIEL   I had to file a police report.

DENISE   You did?

DANIEL   Of course I did.

Beat.

DENISE   You're upset.

DANIEL   UPSET?! You have no idea, not a clue how... how...
          Screw this, I'm going to stay at a hotel!

He starts packing an overnight bag.

DENISE   I'm sorry, okay? I am... Don't go, Daniel, please?

DANIEL   Please what?

DENISE   Can we not talk about this?

DANIEL   What.

Silence. She reaches for him. He pulls away.

Don't.

DENISE   I said I was sorry.

DANIEL   Not good enough.

DENISE   Daniel—

DANIEL   I had to file a missing persons report.

DENISE   I know.

Silence. She starts to sing.

"You are my sunshine—"

DANIEL   Don't.

Beat.

DENISE   "My only sunshine—"

She moves in closer.

DANIEL   Seriously, stop it.

A long and painful silence.

DENISE   You're right. You deserve better. I'm sorry.

She holds out her hand. He hesitates and then grabs it. They embrace.

DANIEL   I'm still angry—

DENISE   I know—

DANIEL   A phone call—

DENISE   A phone call—

DANIEL   That's all I need—

DENISE   I know—

DANIEL   I know you know… I thought I lost you.

DENISE   Sorry, but you're going to have to work a lot harder than that to get rid of me.

DANIEL   Well, maybe you need to start working a lot harder to keep me.

DENISE   Ouch.

DANIEL   You deserve it.

DENISE   Fair enough. Well at least let me try to make it up to you.

DANIEL   It's not that easy, love.

DENISE   At least let me try?

DANIEL   Dee.

DENISE   Please.

Beat.

DANIEL   Fine. What do you have in mind?

DENISE   Oh, I don't know… I thought maybe a bottle of wine…

DANIEL   Uh huh.

DENISE   And some nudity later on?

Beat.

DANIEL   *(contemplates her offer)* It's a start.

They kiss.

DENISE   Daniel.

DANIEL   Yeah?

DENISE   Go grab the wine.

He goes to run off but stops himself.

DANIEL   Is nudity guaranteed, or merely a possibility?

DENISE   Go!

DANIEL   Right. I'll be right back.

He runs off.

DENISE   And don't forget the corkscrew!

MICHELLE *(from off)* Sh, sh. Keep it down, eh?

A woman enters wearing a hoodie and jeans.

DENISE   Michelle.

MICHELLE   Respect for the fallen.

DENISE   The fallen?

MICHELLE   Yeah, you don't want to be disturbing the spirits, eh?

DENISE   No. No of course not.

MICHELLE   You don't have a bit of change, do you?

DENISE   Uh, yeah, I think so.

              DENISE reaches into her pocket and gives her some.

              Sorry, it's not much.

MICHELLE   Hey that's all right. Every bit helps, eh?

DENISE   Sure.

MICHELLE   It's chilly out. Temperature is going to drop tonight.

DENISE   You look cold.

MICHELLE   It's nothing. I walk down here all the time, eh? It
              feels detached from the rest of the city. People always
              say, "Wow, I didn't know this place was down here."
              That's why the girls come here, eh? Hurts my heart.
              Sometimes I try to count them but there's too many
              now. All them girls, all of them lost. But a sad lost, you
              know? Like you could show them the way home but
              they wouldn't go because they're too ashamed of what
              happened to them. I try not to think about it too much.

DENISE   Have you talked to the police?

MICHELLE   They flew me in, lots of us, years ago. No jobs, no future, and people were getting sick from the water. I didn't want to go, but my gram said there was no use fighting 'em, that it would only make things worse. So I went. I was going to go to school but that didn't happen, so I ended up here. I want to go back home but it's hard to leave this place once it gets inside of you.

DENISE   How long have you been out here?

MICHELLE   Oh I don't know, I'm starting to forget dates. It's hard to keep them straight in my head... It's the first thing to go, you know? Makes it easier I guess... '81.

DENISE   Nineteen eighty-one?

MICHELLE   Yeah, sounds right. Feels right.

DENISE   That was a long time ago.

MICHELLE   Yeah, I think I was the first from here to go missing.

DENISE   Sorry?

MICHELLE   Maybe the second? I can't remember now. Memories, eh? Slippery like a fish.

DENISE   Michelle, I'm confused.

MICHELLE   Ooooo, names are the same as dates. They erode away, you know?

DENISE   Michelle it's me, Denise.

MICHELLE Denise… Michelle… Michelle sounds familiar. I might have met her. Where was your Michelle murdered?

DENISE faints. The lights extinguish like someone blacking out. Lights up again sharply. Enter DANIEL. He goes over to wake DENISE up.

DANIEL Rise and shine, sleepy head. You're wasting away the day. Denise.

DENISE *(wakes up)* What?

DANIEL It's past noon. You never sleep in. Coffee's on.

DENISE Where am I?

DANIEL In bed, silly.

DENISE Oh, Daniel, I've been having the craziest dreams.

DANIEL Really? Was I in them?

DENISE Yeah, and you were angry. It was the first time I went looking for Michelle.

DANIEL Ah, right. I remember that.

DENISE But Michelle was there too.

DANIEL She was?

DENISE It's like I was being given the pieces to a puzzle I had to put together.

DANIEL What do you mean?

DENISE   Do you know where I put my medicines? I have to put down some tobacco.

DENISE gets up and starts looking for her tobacco.

DANIEL   Ah, Dee, maybe you should take a minute. You just woke up.

DENISE   I had a vision.

DANIEL   No, you said it was a dream.

DENISE   She was trying to tell me something.

DANIEL   I understand that, but why don't you take a moment to relax, have some coffee, and then maybe we can figure out what your dreams are trying to tell you.

DENISE   It wasn't a dream; it was a vision.

DANIEL   Okay, it was a vision. I'm just saying that it's unlikely that she—

DENISE   I'm just saying? You're always *just saying* stuff, Daniel.

I hate those words.

DANIEL   Denise. You just woke up. You're talking about a dream you had last night—vision—sorry—vision you had last night. I'm sorry if I'm finding it hard to follow your train of thought right now. I'm just saying that—

DENISE   There you go again—

DANIEL   Denise—

DENISE   You're just saying what? That it's crazy to think that my
              sister came to me in a vision?

DANIEL   Listen, all I'm saying is let's make a rational decision
              after a hot shower and a full breakfast.

DENISE   All I'm saying? That's another one you like to use.

DANIEL   I don't want to fight. I know you want her back. It's hard
              when you're desperate for a sign. Five years is a long
              time to go without any answers, I understand that, but
              a dream or a vision or whatever it was is nothing to hang
              all our hopes on. Even if it feels like it's real. You're just
              starting to find your feet again.

DENISE   I haven't found anything, Daniel. I've lost a part of who
              I am.

DANIEL   I understand that, but we've come so far from where we
              were. I don't think anything that isn't based on fact is
              worth this amount of energy. Let's have some breakfast,
              drink some coffee, and let calmer heads prevail.

DENISE   I am calm.

DANIEL   Would you stop for a second, I'm talking to you.

DENISE   This isn't about you.

DANIEL   I am well aware of that.

DENISE   She was trying to tell me something, Daniel.

DANIEL   I'm sure she was.

DENISE   She was.

DANIEL   Sure.

DENISE   Forget it. Have you seen my medicines?

DANIEL   No.

DENISE   I need to put down some tobacco for her.

DANIEL   NO… they're in the closet.

DENISE   Thanks.

*DENISE leaves. DANIEL is upset. He does not see a woman enter.
She is dishevelled and badly beaten. She can barely walk. She
is in another reality, drawn to something out in front of her as
she crosses the room.*

DANIEL   This isn't going to end, is it?

DENISE   *(from off)* How can you ask me a question like that?

DANIEL   I'm not asking for me.

DENISE   *(from off)* Don't play the martyr, Daniel.

DANIEL   I'm not. If you'd only take a step back—

DENISE   *(from off)* NO. I have to do this.

This upsets DANIEL. He gets up to leave.

DANIEL   Right, of course you do. Please just be careful.

DENISE   *(from off)* Careful of what?

He walks up and addresses MICHELLE *by accident, thinking it is*
DENISE.

DANIEL   I don't know. That's the problem.

MICHELLE *doesn't react, and this upsets him so he leaves.* DENISE
re-enters.

DENISE   You can't do that to me; you can't say something cryptic
              like that to me and then walk away. Mich! Oh I knew
              you'd come back. I was looking for some tobacco to
              put down because I didn't know what else to do. Then
              Daniel and I started to argue—

MICHELLE *is looking out at something. No reply.*

              Are you all right?

MICHELLE *squints into the set of headlights of the car that brought*
her out here. She has been beaten and raped severely and left
lying in a field. She has managed to get herself up on two broken
legs. It takes everything for her to remain standing.

MICHELLE Fourteen.

DENISE   What?

MICHELLE He said I was fourteen.

DENISE   You were fourteen? Who said you were fourteen?

DENISE stops when MICHELLE *turns and acknowledges her for the*
first time with a look. Then she turns back to face him.

MICHELLE   I can't move.

DENISE   Don't worry, I'm here.

MICHELLE   Both my legs are broken. One more step and I'll fall.

DENISE   Let me help you—

MICHELLE   No, you need to run. He's fast. I won't be able to save you. Please, run!

DENISE   I'm not leaving you.

MICHELLE   No, you don't understand. It's not me he's after; it's you! He's here for you!

A flood of sound as if DENISE *is being hit from behind. Blackout.*

Lights up on DENISE *and* DANIEL. *She is on the ground. He is behind her.*

DANIEL   Denise?

DENISE *screams and reacts in self-defence. She is disoriented.*

DENISE   GET AWAY FROM ME, GET AWAY FROM ME!—

DANIEL   —Whoa, whoa, it's me, Daniel!—

DENISE   —Where am I, where have you taken me?—

DANIEL   —Nowhere. You're at the police station, Dee—

DENISE   —The police station?—

DANIEL —Yeah. I'm here to take you home—

DENISE —Michelle?—

DANIEL —No, love, it's me—

DENISE —Where is she? Is she okay?—

DANIEL —I don't know, but I'm here to take you home—

DENISE —Michelle was attacked. I saw it. She's in trouble—

DANIEL —You've been here all night. Here, let's get you up on your feet—

DENISE —She's in a lot of trouble, Daniel. She was attacked—

DANIEL —Well I haven't seen you in over a month, so I don't know anything about that!

Beat.

DENISE Oh, Daniel. I'm sorry, I know I'm supposed to call you, but things keep overlapping in my head and I can't keep them straight anymore. I don't know what's real and what's not.

DANIEL Well, here's the good news: I am real. And, if you want, I can try to help you figure things out… deal?

He bends down and holds his hand out.

DENISE Deal.

Beat. She realizes.

Why am I at the police station?

DANIEL   They picked you up in the mall parking lot. You were yelling at the overnight security staff.

DENISE   Really?

DANIEL   You collapsed so they rushed you to the hospital. Paramedics said you were severely malnourished and dehydrated. Since when are you not taking care of yourself?

DENISE   I am taking care of myself, thank you very much.

MICHELLE enters. DANIEL does not see her.

MICHELLE You were doing it on purpose.

DENISE   I was? Michelle! Thank goodness you're okay.

DANIEL   Sorry?

MICHELLE You were fasting. You wanted more visions to appear.

DENISE   That's right, I was fasting.

DANIEL   You were what?

MICHELLE Remember when Gram used to tell us stories about it when we were kids?

DENISE   Yeah. I didn't know what else to do. Wait, Daniel, you said they took me to the hospital.

DANIEL   Yeah.

DENISE   Then why are we at the police station?

DANIEL   Well… you fought the paramedics in the ambulance, took on several of the nurses at the reception desk, and then slapped the emergency-room doctor trying to examine you. Let's just say you were attended to and then subsequently released to the police.

MICHELLE   I'm impressed.

DENISE   Me too. Wow. I told you she was real.

DANIEL   Who?

DENISE   Michelle, silly.

DANIEL   Look, you're tired. Let's get you up and out of here.

He goes to help her up.

DENISE   Ow, I'm sore.

MICHELLE   Easy on her now.

DANIEL   I can't imagine why. Take it slow.

He gets her up on her feet.

Can you walk to the car?

DENISE   Michelle, are you coming?

DANIEL   Denise.

DENISE   Yeah?

DANIEL   You're starting to worry me now. Michelle's not here. It's just me, Daniel.

DENISE   Michelle?

MICHELLE Don't worry, I'm coming.

DENISE   Daniel, seriously, you can't see her?

DANIEL   Denise. Lets just get you home.

All of them exit the stage. Lights to black. It is night again. We hear the sounds of a country ditch. A transport truck drives by.

MICHELLE Pst… it's me. I'm lying in the grass somewhere along the highway. I can't move. I want to call for help, but I can't get the words out. Hey, the big dipper's out tonight.

The big dipper appears.

          I can't seem to stay awake. The transports shake the ground when they pass so it keeps me from drifting off too long. I'm not going to lie to you, I'm in pretty rough shape. I can't feel my legs, and my ribs feel like they're broken. I wish you were here, I really do. But, it's probably best that you didn't see me like this. Hey, the crickets are out.

We hear the crickets.

          They've all come down to see me off. Well, at least that's what I'm telling myself.

Everything fades to black and silence for the last line.

This will be my last breath… This will be my last breath…

This will be my last breath… Please let this be my last breath.

Lights up. DENISE *sits with a bunch of folders in front of her.* DANIEL *is sitting off on the side. She starts pulling out her folders and papers.*

DENISE   So I started looking into other missing women in this area, and you would not believe how many there are. Staggering, actually; like, it made me sick there were so many names.

DANIEL   Dee, you promised not tonight—

DENISE   Don't— You started this. You think I'm crazy then listen to this: Laney Menard's car was found two kilometres from where Michelle's was found. Two kilometres! That's not very far. She was a lawyer just like the woman in my vision. What do you have to say about that?

DANIEL   I thought we were going to take it easy tonight—

DENISE   In this article it says her mother walked that stretch of highway for three years looking for her. They say you can still see her out there some days.

DANIEL   Uh huh.

DENISE   Loraine Major was homeless when she went missing. Now, it was hard to find anything about her but I did find an article from the *Free Press* about a shelter

volunteer that had contacted police about the disappearance of a young woman named Loraine. She was
last seen wearing a red hoodie just like the girl in my
vision. Get this: The police wouldn't investigate because
no one could prove she had actually gone missing. So
no missing-persons report was ever filed. She just disappeared. See?

DANIEL   See what?

DENISE   It wasn't a dream.

DANIEL   Dee, please—

DENISE   Sandra Williams was a prostitute just like the woman in
my vision. Her daughter went into foster care when she
went missing. Sandra had worked the streets for years
and was like a mom to a lot of the girls out there. When
she disappeared, the police were inundated with phone
calls from women trying to report her missing. Police
blamed her high-risk lifestyle and nothing was made of
her disappearance. Like, nothing! Can you believe that?

DANIEL   Uh huh.

DENISE   High-risk lifestyle—I'll tell you what that means; it
means poverty. All of these women deserved better.

DANIEL   Why are we talking about this right now?

DENISE   Because I think they're connected to Michelle's disappearance. I just don't know how yet.

DANIEL   Did they give you their names?

DENISE   No.

DANIEL   Then I don't see the point of this.

DENISE   Daniel—

DANIEL   No, I'm sorry, but a lot of these details are fairly general.
                You said it yourself, there's not a lot to go on. I bet you
                could come up with a whole list of women who fit the
                exact same description.

DENISE   I know, it's sad, isn't it?

DANIEL   Yes it is. But do we have to go through this now?

DENISE   That lawyer, Laney Menard, she used a pay phone to
                report her car stolen the night she disappeared. Explain
                that to me.

DANIEL   Explain what?

DENISE   Why it matches my vision. Or what about the prostitute
                Sandra Williams? She actually mothered me. She even
                mentioned her daughter!

DANIEL   Cars are stolen all the time, and there's a lot of missing
                sex workers out there.

DENISE   Daniel, she was a human being.

DANIEL   I know, but you can't deny the fact that it's a high-risk
                lifestyle.

DENISE   Please don't marginalize them like that.

DANIEL   I'm not. I just don't think the police intended any malice
           when they said that stuff. It's the unfortunate reality in
           dealing with these kinds of people.

MICHELLE enters. DANIEL *does not see who he is talking to.*

MICHELLE   These kinds of people?!

DANIEL   You know what I mean.

MICHELLE   No I don't.

DENISE   Michelle!

DANIEL   Michelle?

He looks up and sees MICHELLE.

MICHELLE   Don't listen to him.

DENISE   See, I told you she was real.

DANIEL   Who?

DENISE   Michelle.

DANIEL   Oh, please, can we not do this again.

MICHELLE   You ready to go?

DANIEL   I thought we were taking it easy tonight.

MICHELLE   We have to go to the Mill Rock.

DENISE   You can't see her?

DANIEL   No, can you?

MICHELLE   What is all this?

DENISE   These are my files of all the women who have gone missing in the area. I didn't find much, mostly just names, lots and lots of names.

DANIEL   I know, I know. But you promised me you wouldn't do this tonight.

DENISE   But this is—

DANIEL   —Is a job for the police. If these women were connected in any way, I'm sure they would have found something by now.

MICHELLE   You are unbelievable!

DENISE   Please, I don't want to fight right now.

DANIEL   Me neither.

MICHELLE   Good, it's settled then. Can we get going?

DANIEL   I know you want to find her, and I want to support you in that.

DENISE   And I appreciate that.

MICHELLE   Here comes the "but"—

DANIEL   —But... Um... What are you expecting to find here?

MICHELLE   He doesn't get it.

DENISE   I don't know, but I have to follow this through.

DANIEL   So, it doesn't matter what I think?

MICHELLE   No, because this isn't about you.

DENISE   Of course it matters, but I've got to do this.

DANIEL   Right now?

DENISE   Yes, right now.

DANIEL   You promised you would take the night off.

MICHELLE   Oh get over yourself.

DANIEL   We don't spend enough time together anymore.

DENISE   I know, I know, and we will. Tomorrow, I promise, just
              you and me, okay?

Beat.

DANIEL   Okay… I don't want to lose you again.

DENISE   I know.

DANIEL   No, I don't think you do.

He kisses her and leaves.

MICHELLE   Aaaaaaaaaand… goodbye.

*DENISE gives MICHELLE a look and then starts to clean up the
papers.*

What?

DENISE   Nothing.

MICHELLE   You have that look in your eyes. What?

DENISE   It's too much sometimes.

MICHELLE   I know. You really have to walk away when he gets like that.

DENISE   I'm talking about you.

MICHELLE   You've got to be kidding me, right?

DENISE   No, I'm serious.

MICHELLE   We are this close and he pulls that on you.

DENISE   He didn't pull anything. This is hard on him.

MICHELLE   Well, I humbly disagree. And I'm your sister, so deal with it.

DENISE   Right.

MICHELLE   Daniel needs to let things be.

Beat.

DENISE   Sorry, what did you just say?

MICHELLE   I said he needs to let it be.

DENISE   Oh. Funny that.

MICHELLE Funny what?

DENISE I just remembered a dream I had about you last night.

MICHELLE Oh yeah?

DENISE Yeah.

MICHELLE Did it involve me strangling your husband?

DENISE No.

MICHELLE Damn.

DENISE No, it was the middle of the night and I was standing outside in the snow. The sky was moonless so it was pitch black and cold, but, like, January cold. I couldn't see where I was. I tried to reach out for something but there was nothing to grab on to. It felt like I was going to disappear or something and so I started to panic. And then I heard something, like a murmur... It was the sound of shuffling feet. It came closer, then moved farther back, and then closer again, but always in rhythm. I couldn't see anything, yet the footsteps never ceased. And then, quick like a sneeze, it lit up like a can of gasoline thrown on a fire. And I saw off in the distance: it was a woman dancing. She was dressed in full regalia and it was completely engulfed in flames, every piece of it. I panicked. I ran towards her. I tried to grab onto her and throw her to the ground, but she kept dancing, kept moving away from me. It was like I couldn't reach her no matter how hard I tried. Then I saw her face. It was you. You gave me this look, and you said, "This is how it was meant to be, so let it be." So I did. In the

black of night I stood in the snow and you danced away
the dark… and I felt safe, safer than I'd felt in a long
time.

MICHELLE   Hmm. That is quite the dream.

DENISE   What does it mean?

MICHELLE   Sorry, kiddo. You have to do that one on your own.

DENISE   Please?

MICHELLE   Just keep doing what you're doing. You'll figure it out.

DENISE   I've been to the Mill Rock turnoff a dozen times. I don't
know what I'm looking for. I need your help.

MICHELLE   Dee, I can't.

DENISE   Why not?

MICHELLE   Listen… there are things I can't tell you, but what I can
say is this—

DENISE   —Michelle?

MICHELLE   What?

DENISE   Michelle? Where did you go?

MICHELLE   I'm right here.

DENISE   Stop playing around.

MICHELLE   Denise, I'm right here.

DENISE   Where are you? Michelle?

MICHELLE   Oh no.

DENISE   Michelle? I don't feel so good. What's going on?

MICHELLE   Listen to me! Go to the Mill Rock turnoff. It's there, you'll see it! I promise.

DENISE   Michelle!

MICHELLE   I'm going to try and find Daniel. I'll be right back!

MICHELLE turns to leave as DANIEL enters.

He addresses MICHELLE like it was DENISE.

DANIEL   Does this feel like the right spot to you?

DENISE   Daniel?

He realizes his mistake.

DANIEL   Oh. Uhm. Sorry, I thought—

DENISE   I'm not feeling very well.

DANIEL   Yeah, this place gives me the willies. Sorry, what are we looking for again?

DENISE   I don't know.

DANIEL   You don't know what we're looking for?

DENISE   My sister.

DANIEL   Yeah, I get that part, but what in particular?

DENISE   I don't know. I think I have to sit down.

DANIEL   This feels like a big waste of time.

DENISE   Stop being like that.

DANIEL   Sorry, but we're out here for the umpteenth time look-
             ing for I don't know, and you say you don't know, so, yes,
             I'm being like "this" because I'm frustrated.

DENISE   Then why did you come out here?

DANIEL   Because I didn't want you out here alone!

DENISE   Thanks!

DANIEL   You're welcome!

DENISE   Right!

DANIEL   Sure!

   A long silence. Then he walks over to her.

             So, where should we start?

DENISE   I don't know. Let's start over there.

   DENISE leads the way as she exits. DANIEL goes to follow.

MICHELLE   Daniel?

   DANIEL stops. Beat.

Daniel, please.

DANIEL   What?

MICHELLE   Stop pretending you can't see me.

DANIEL   I'm not.

MICHELLE   Then look at me and say that.

He deliberately looks at her then turns away.

DANIEL   Leave us alone, Michelle, please?

MICHELLE   This isn't right.

DANIEL   No, everything is fine. She's come back to me.

MICHELLE   No she hasn't. She's lost, Daniel, that's how she ended up here.

DANIEL   What are you talking about?

MICHELLE   This, all of this—it's not real.

DANIEL   How can you say that? You and I are standing here talking. This isn't real?

MICHELLE   Daniel, I'm dead. That should be your first clue that something is wrong here. You're going to have to let her go.

DANIEL   Why?

MICHELLE   Because you have to.

DANIEL   I can't.

MICHELLE   Can't what?

DANIEL   Let her go. I did it once and I won't do it again.

MICHELLE   Daniel, I know what I'm asking is unfair, but it's the only way we can save her.

DANIEL   No, listen, maybe we can figure this out. If you stayed too—

MICHELLE   She will leave here like she came and there is nothing you can do about it. And if you don't help her now, you will return to your life but she won't. She will remain neither here nor there.

DANIEL   If you're dead then why are you here?

MICHELLE   I am her connection to death, Daniel, and you are her connection to life. I've come to help her. Don't you want to help her?

DANIEL   Of course I do.

MICHELLE   Then you need to ask Denise what these numbers mean to her. First maybe second, three, nine, fourteen, seventeen.

DENISE enters out of breath.

DENISE   Hey, I was at the turnoff. I was walking down the hill and I stumbled across a memorial of some kind at the bottom. I've never seen it before. Then I found another one on the other side down by the river.

MICHELLE   Please ask her.

DANIEL   What if you're wrong?

MICHELLE   I'm not wrong.

DENISE   I can't believe I didn't see them before.

DANIEL   I can't.

MICHELLE   If you don't ask her I will haunt you for the rest of your life!

DENISE   Maybe that's what I was meant to find... What?

MICHELLE   Daniel!

DANIEL   No. I can't risk it.

He looks around. He can't see DENISE *anymore.*

Denise? Denise!

The reality of this world begins to crumble. The shifts are fast and brief.

DENISE   Stop fooling. Where did you go?

MICHELLE   *(She loses* DANIEL.*)* Daniel?

DENISE   *(to* MICHELLE*)* Michelle!

MICHELLE   *(to* DENISE*)* Dee! You can see me?

DENISE   *(to* MICHELLE*)* Yes, of course. Are you okay?

MICHELLE   Yeah, listen to me— Daniel!

DANIEL   *(to MICHELLE)* I lost her. She disappeared right in front
            of my eyes.

MICHELLE   *(looking around for DENISE)* She did the same to me just
            now.

DANIEL   What do we do?—

MICHELLE   So do you believe me now?

DANIEL   —How do I help her?

DENISE   *(She loses MICHELLE.)* Michelle?

MICHELLE   *(to DANIEL)* You need to ask her what those numbers
            mean to her.

DANIEL   What are the numbers again?

DENISE   *(She sees DANIEL.)* Daniel. Where's Michelle? I just saw her.

DANIEL   *(He finds DENISE but loses MICHELLE.)* She's with me. You
            need to hear this—

MICHELLE   *(She is lost.)* Hello?

DENISE   *(She is lost.)* Daniel?

DANIEL   *(He is lost.)* Denise?

MICHELLE   Daniel!

DANIEL   *(He finds MICHELLE.)* What are the numbers?!

MICHELLE _(to DANIEL)_ First maybe second—

DANIEL Uh huh.

MICHELLE Three, nine—

DENISE _(finds DANIEL)_ There you are!

MICHELLE & DANIEL _(lose each other)_ Dammit!

DENISE _(to DANIEL)_ Where were you?

DANIEL _(to DENISE)_ I've been here the whole time. Michelle was just with me. Dee?

DENISE She was?

MICHELLE _(She finds DENISE.)_ Dee! Listen to me, we don't have much time.

DANIEL _(He loses DENISE.)_ Please, please, where are you?

MICHELLE First maybe second, three, nine—

DENISE _(to MICHELLE)_ What?

MICHELLE _(frustrated)_ Ahhh!

DANIEL _(He finds MICHELLE.)_ Michelle, what are the numbers again?

MICHELLE _(to DANIEL)_ First maybe second, three, nine, fourteen, seventeen.

DANIEL _(to MICHELLE)_ First maybe second, three, nine, fourteen—

MICHELLE —Seventeen—

DANIEL What?!

MICHELLE Seventeen!

DANIEL Dammit.

DENISE Daniel?

DANIEL Hey, does this mean anything to you? First maybe second, three, nine, fourteen… uh.

DENISE I don't know, why?

MICHELLE They're important.

DANIEL Michelle says they're important.

DENISE First maybe second…

DANIEL Yeah.

DENISE Three, nine, fourteen…

MICHELLE Seventeen!

DANIEL Seventeen! Have you heard those numbers before?

DENISE I don't know. I mean…

It hits her. She pulls out the piece of paper and reads it.

Nine! She handed it to me… I thought it was… but it must be… First maybe second… three, nine… She said... fourteen! Michelle said fourteen. I thought she was talking about her age... First maybe second... Oh... That's it, Daniel! The homeless girl Loraine said she was the first, maybe the second... They're numbered. He numbered his victims. If Loraine was the first, maybe the second, victim, and Sandra was nine, Michelle, fourteen... Then who was... wait... I think the lawyer said... She did! Laney said she was three. First maybe second, three, nine, fourteen. All the numbers except one. Who is seventeen? Who is seventeen?

MICHELLE   Tell her.

DANIEL   Wait.

MICHELLE   Daniel, please. This is it.

DANIEL   I know, okay? I know. Just give me a second.

MICHELLE   Daniel.

DANIEL   Denise?

DENISE   What?

DANIEL   Dee, I need to tell you something—

DENISE   —Maybe I'm meant to save her—

DANIEL   —Listen, you can't save her—

DENISE   —You can be so cynical sometimes—

DANIEL   —It was you—

DENISE   —Shouldn't I at least try—

DANIEL   —Dee, It was you—

DENISE   —This is a woman's life we're talking about here—

DANIEL   —Denise, you were seventeen!

DENISE   What?

DANIEL   You were seventeen!

Beat.

DENISE   What do you mean?

DANIEL   When Michelle went missing, when she disappeared, you dedicated your life to finding her. There was nothing else, not me, not anything. Our life was over.

DENISE   That's not true.

DANIEL   I never knew where you were. You'd be gone for weeks at a time. It killed me, but I did my best to support you because, well… because. Then one day the police showed up at my work. They had found your car abandoned on the highway.

DENISE   What do you mean?

DANIEL   I never saw you again. I tried to find you. I did. I looked everywhere… but… I lost you. So I came home. And there to greet me were all of your things. All of our pictures on the fridge, your books by the bed, and that jar of mismatching chopsticks. And your plants—you'd be impressed—I somehow managed to keep them alive. Now I'm afraid to lose them. And I don't know why but I keep making dinner for two… And it happened so fast. Your smell was gone from all of your clothes, and your pillow. And I would always use your favourite shampoo in the shower 'cause I could close my eyes and it smelled like you there with me…

About a month ago I walked into the kitchen and there you were, standing in your bathrobe. Singing without a care in the world like the last two years hadn't happened. I didn't know what to do so I stayed awake that night in case I was dreaming. But the next day you stayed, and then the next day came, and the next, and I kept on pretending like this was the way things had always been.

DENISE   I don't understand.

DANIEL   I didn't want to lose you again… so I didn't tell you.

I just wanted you to stay.

Silence. He can't see her anymore.

Denise? Denise!

DENISE   Daniel?

MICHELLE   Heya.

DENISE   Michelle!

DENISE *runs up to her sister and hugs her.*

Is it true?

MICHELLE Yeah. It's time for us to go.

DENISE Where are we going?

MICHELLE Where we need to.

DANIEL Denise, please come back.

DENISE Daniel, what's wrong?

MICHELLE He can't see you anymore.

DENISE Why?

MICHELLE Because, he had to let you go.

DENISE Daniel.

MICHELLE Dee, this is how it was meant to be, so let it be.

DENISE My dream.

MICHELLE Yes.

Looks back.

The light? It's for you.

We see the flash of lights like lightning bugs, hundreds of them that form into a pool of warm light.

DANIEL Please, Dee?

MICHELLE   Now it's your turn.

DENISE   My turn?

MICHELLE   Yes. You have to let go too. That's how we pass over.

DENISE   Really?

MICHELLE   Yeah. Think of it as letting it all go so you can take it all with you.

DENISE   Can he hear me?

MICHELLE   No, I'm sorry.

DENISE   Daniel. Oh, Daniel, I didn't know how much I had hurt you. You deserved better.

MICHELLE   Dee.

DENISE   It's true. I couldn't have found her without you, my love.

MICHELLE   …Sing for him. Music is the only thing that can be heard in the passage between life and death. He'll hear it. Meegwetch, Daniel. Chi Meegwetch… Sing.

DENISE   Everything is going to be okay.

DENISE begins to sing as they take the long road home. As the song continues we start to hear other women's voices added until it is a chorus of voices.

"You are my sunshine,
My only sunshine.

DANIEL *hears the song.*

> You make me happy when skies are grey.

DANIEL *begins to sing too.*

> You'll never know, dear, how much I love you.
> Oh please don't take my sunshine away.
> The other night, dear, as I lay sleeping, I dreamed I held you in my arms.
> When I awoke, dear,

DANIEL *struggles but cannot find the words to finish as the chorus of women begins to fade like they are passing over.*

> I was mistaken, and I hung my head and cried.
> You are my sunshine, my only sunshine.
> you make me happy… when skies are grey.
> …you'll never know, dear… how much I love you…"

The lights fade to black and the voices do the same shortly after.

The end.

OPTIONAL ENDING IN THE BLACKOUT

We hear the faint sound of a crowd of people, followed by a burst of celebration. Like when someone you haven't seen in a long time walks into a room full of family and friends. It's in the warmth of celebration that we fade to black.

ACKNOWLEDGEMENTS

To my mom, my sisters, and my family: my love to you all. I wouldn't
be the artist I am today if it wasn't for all of you. My sincere gratitude
to the workshop actors—Michaela Washburn, Paula-Jean Prudat,
Eli Ham, Michelle Pollock, Sharmila Day, and Keira Loughran. For
your generosity and care with my script. For your questions and clar-
ity with the story. To New Harlem Productions and Saskatchewan
Native Theatre Company for producing the play. To Curtis and Alan
and Donna-Michelle, who did all the legwork to get us on the stage.
To Native Earth Performing Arts and Yvette Nolan for giving me a
home to work on this play. And to Tara Beagan who continued to
nurture me as a writer when she took over as artistic director. So
many friends to thank, but special thanks to Marcus, Karen, Wade,
Steven, Jackie, Rod, Mary Beth, Michelle, Joshua & Carol, and Jerry.
To Genne, who had to live with me during the writing of this, and
to Hoito, who forced me to go outside to get some much-needed
fresh air. To Mr. David Storch, who was the absolute best director
a playwright could ask for, but also an inspiring artist and friend.
To Leah-Simone for her advice when I needed it. To all the people
who worked on the production: Erin Birkenberg who put in a lot of
long hours, to Richard who ran the ship, Isidra who designed the
costumes, Monique who choreographed the most difficult part of
the play, Andy Moro for his beautiful set and projection design, the
lovely Michelle Ramsay who designed the lighting, Samuel Sholdice
who built a beautiful soundscape for the play, Jennifer Dawn Bisop
and Arron Naytowhow who came all the way from Saskatoon to be
in the room with us, and Aaron Shingoose who assisted Richard
and was our backstage helper. A big thank you to my dramaturges
Isaac Thomas and Donna-Michelle St. Bernard—Isaac, who came
in with a fresh set of eyes and forced me to write what I was afraid
to write, and Donna-Michelle, who was the first person to tell me I
was a playwright and has always been my biggest supporter and rock

throughout this journey. Meegwetch times four to the Creator and the ancestors for getting me to this place. And finally, to the loveliest person I have ever met, Catherine Butler. My heart is yours. You really are the wonder that keeps the stars apart. X

The writing and development of this play was financially supported by project funding through the Ontario Arts Council, the Toronto Arts Council, and the Canada Council for the Arts, including a Toronto Arts Council Level 1 Playwright Grant and from the Ontario Arts Council Theatre Creators Reserve Program, via a recommendation by Magnus Theatre. Additional contributions toward development were made through the Weesageechak Festival via Native Earth Performing Arts, the Métis Nation of Ontario, and the SpringWorks Festival. Funds were also made available through an Indiegogo campaign. Thank you to Alex Maveal, my uncle Tom, Bobby Theodore, my sister Bryce, Paul and Bev Turpin, Cathy Mac, Christine Horne, Christine Rambukkana, Cole J. Alvis, Eric Grimstead, Freya Ravensbergen, Jared Peck, Kevin George, Krystal Meadows, Laurel Koop, Lisa Cook Ravensbergen, Marcus Lundgren, Margaret Evans, Margaret Keenan, Mark Cassidy, Mary Shrock, Natalie Robitaille, Nina Lee Aquino, Nadine Shuster, my mom, Yvette Nolan, Anonymous, xiaolaisa, and navigator12_53.

Keith Barker is a Metis actor and a playwright from Northwestern Ontario. He graduated from the George Brown Theatre School, moving on to become Artistic Associate at Native Earth Performing Arts. Currently he is the playwright-in-residence at Native Earth for the 2012/13 season. *The Hours That Remain* is his first full-length play.

Printed on Rolland Enviro, which contains 100% post-consumer fiber, is ECOLOGO, Processed Chlorine Free, Ancient Forest Friendly and FSC® certified and is manufactured using renewable biogas energy.

PERMANENT

100%

Ancient Forest Friendly™